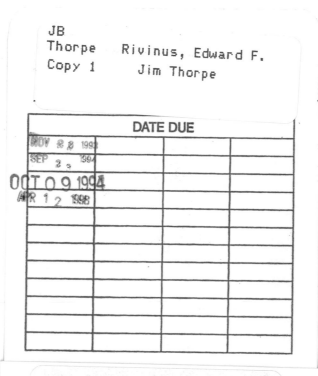

To the Reader . . .

The **Raintree/Rivilo American Indian Stories** series features the lives of American Indian men and women important in the history of their tribes. Our purpose is to provide young readers with accurate accounts of the lives of these individuals. The stories are written by scholars, including American Indians.

Indians are as much a part of American life today as they were one hundred years ago. Even in times past, Indians were not all the same. Not all of them lived in tepees or wore feather warbonnets. They were not all warriors. Some did fight against the white man, but many befriended him.

Whether patriot or politician, athlete or artist, Arapaho or Zuni, the story of each person in this series deserves to be told. Whether the individuals gained distinction on the battlefield or the playing field, in the courtroom or the classroom, they have enriched the heritage and history of all Americans. It is hoped that those who read their stories will realize that many different peoples, regardless of culture or color, have played a part in shaping the United States, in making America the great country that it is today.

Herman J. Viola
General Editor
Author of *Exploring the West*
and other volumes on the West
and American Indians

GENERAL EDITOR

Herman J. Viola

Author of *Exploring the West* and other volumes on the West and American Indians

MANAGING EDITOR

Robert M. Kvasnicka

Coeditor of *The Commissioners of Indian Affairs, 1824–1977*
Coeditor of *Indian-White Relations: A Persistent Paradox*

MANUSCRIPT EDITOR

Barbara J. Behm

DESIGNER

Kathleen A. Hartnett

PRODUCTION

Andrew Rupniewski
Eileen Rickey

First Steck-Vaughn Edition 1992

Copyright © 1990 Pinnacle Press, Inc. doing business as Rivilo Books

Library of Congress Number: 89-10457

  3 4 5 6 7 8 9   97 96 95 94 93 92

Library of Congress Cataloging-in-Publication Data

Rivinus, Edward F.
    Jim Thorpe.
    (Raintree American Indian stories)
    Summary: Examines the life of the American Indian who earned fame as one of the nation's greatest all-round athletes.
    1. Thorpe, Jim, 1887-1953—Juvenile literature. 2. Athletes—United States—Biography—Juvenile literature. 3. Athletes, Indian—Biography—Juvenile literature. 4. Indians of North America—Biography—Juvenile literature. [1. Thorpe, Jim, 1887-1953.
2. Athletes. 3. Indians of North America—Biography.] I. Title.
II. Series.
GV697.T5R58 1989   796'.092   [B] [92]   89-10457
ISBN 0-8172-3403-9 (lib. bdg.)

AMERICAN INDIAN STORIES

JIM THORPE

Text by Edward F. Rivinus
Illustrations by Bob Masheris

RAINTREE
STECK-VAUGHN
L I B R A R Y
Austin, Texas

In 1912, the king of Sweden called him "the greatest athlete in the world." In 1950, an Associated Press poll named him the best athlete of the past fifty years. He was Jim Thorpe, a mixed blood Sauk and Fox Indian from Oklahoma, whose athletic abilities brought him a life of fame and controversy.

Even the date of Jim Thorpe's birth is controversial. Most published sources state that he and his twin brother, Charles, were born in May 1888. School records indicate that they were born in 1887. Jim's mother named him *Wa-Tho-Hack,* which means "Bright Path." She was a member of the Potawatomi tribe, but she had blood ties with the Kickapoo tribe. Her father was a French-Canadian trapper and hunter. Jim's father was the son of an Irish blacksmith, who had come to live among the Indians, and a Sauk and Fox woman, who was said to be a descendant of the great Sauk chief, Black Hawk.

Jim's first home was a one-room cabin made of cottonwood and pecan tree logs. It was located near the North Canadian River on the Sauk and Fox reservation in what was then Indian Territory. Jim's father raised horses and farmed enough to raise food for his family and livestock. He showed Jim and Charles how to hunt, fish, and how to handle horses and other animals.

Jim's father could speak and write English, and he believed in education. When Jim and Charles were six years old, he enrolled them at the Indian agency boarding school. The Indian schools taught Indian children how to live like whites. All of the children had to speak English. Use of their Indian language was forbidden. The students divided their time between studies and working on the school farm.

Charles liked the school, but Jim had trouble fitting in. He wasn't a good student, and the school had no organized sports programs. The students made up their own games, and Jim discovered that he was good at wrestling, running, and jumping. But that didn't make up for his loss of freedom. He preferred to be free to hunt and fish. When he got old enough to do some of the heavy chores at the school, he started running away. His father would whip him and take him back.

In the winter of 1897, Charles died of pneumonia. Jim felt a tremendous loss. He had lost not only a brother but his best friend.

Because Jim would not stay at the Sauk and Fox boarding school, his father sent him to Haskell Institute, a large Indian school in Kansas, three hundred miles from his home. Haskell was run like a military school, but the boys also played football and baseball, games Jim quickly learned. He also learned how important football could be when the Carlisle football team stopped at Haskell for a visit in January 1899.

The Carlisle Indian Industrial School, located in Pennsylvania, had become well known for its athletic program. The football team was on its way home from California where it had won the championship "East-West" game. All the Haskell students were excited and proud that an Indian team had won the championship. In honor of the Carlisle team, Haskell students held a special dress parade and inspection.

In 1901, Jim's father became ill, and Jim decided to leave Haskell to be with him. By the time Jim arrived, his father was well but angry that Jim had run away from yet another school. He beat Jim severely, and this time Jim left his family to live in Texas for a time. Upon his return, he learned that his mother had died.

In 1904, Jim's father sent him to Carlisle. Indian students from different tribes all over the United States came to the school. The boys took courses in trades such as mechanics, tailoring, baking, and farming. The girls were instructed in sewing, cooking, and other domestic arts. Some business courses were also offered. It was a good school, and many Carlisle graduates went on to careers in business, law, and other professions.

Jim stayed at Carlisle, but for the first couple of years he wasn't very happy. He especially disliked the "outing" system, in which the school arranged for the students to spend their vacations living with white families in the area. They were supposed to learn what it was like to live in white homes and to work at various jobs for wages. Many of the farmers, however, treated the students like servants. Jim ran away from the farms. When he got back to school, he was punished, usually by being confined to the guardhouse.

Jim liked Carlisle sports, particularly baseball. He was good at all the games—especially those requiring running and jumping. One day he saw some students trying to jump over a high bar. He asked if he could try, and he cleared the bar easily. When the coach, Glenn S. (Pop) Warner, heard about the jump, he suggested that Jim try out for the football team. During one of his first practices, Jim carried the ball and dodged through the whole squad without anyone being able to tackle him.

The rules of football were very different in those days, and Pop Warner was able to invent and use many tricky plays. Some of these were necessary because the Indian players usually were not as large physically as their white opponents. One play that Warner used only once had the quarterback taking the ball from the center and quickly hiding it under the jersey of one of the other backs. Pop also had fake half footballs sewn on the jerseys of the Carlisle players to confuse the other teams. That ploy was made illegal, but not before Carlisle had scored a number of touchdowns. Coach Warner also was one of the first to use the forward pass. His teams were so well trained that they beat all the large college teams of the day.

During his summer vacation in 1909, Jim went with some of his Carlisle friends to Rocky Mount, North Carolina, where he was hired to play on a semi-pro baseball team. He didn't get paid very much—only $25 to $35 per week—but it was more than he could get doing farm work, and it was fun. Jim's decision to play semi-pro ball was eventually to cause him great grief and to cost him dearly.

At the end of that baseball season, Jim went back home to Oklahoma. He didn't feel like going back to the discipline and studies required by Carlisle—sports or no sports. He spent the year helping his sister on her farm, hunting, fishing, and doing as he pleased. When summer came, he went back to North Carolina where he played a second season of semi-pro baseball.

Some of Jim's football friends from Carlisle began urging him to return to school. Then one day he received a letter from Coach Warner. Pop told Jim that if he returned to Carlisle, he would help Jim train for the United States Olympic track team. The Olympic Games were to be held in Sweden in 1912.

The 1911 football season was one of Carlisle's very best. The Indians beat all the best college teams in the East. The big game of the season was against Harvard. In the last quarter, the score was tied, 15-15, with nine of Carlisle's points coming from field goals Jim had kicked. Carlisle faced fourth down nearly at midfield. To everybody's surprise, the quarterback called for a placekick. Jim stood way back, took a run, and kicked—just in the nick of time as the Harvard blockers rushed in. The ball sailed all the way down the field and over the bar. The final score was Carlisle 18, Harvard 15, and Jim was the hero.

Greater triumphs were to come. Pop Warner was as good as his word. In June, Jim and a Hopi student named Tewanima began to train for the Olympic team. Both made the team, Tewanima as a distance runner and Jim in events more demanding—the decathlon and the pentathlon.

In those days, athletes in the decathlon competed in ten different events over a three-day period—the 100-meter dash, a 400-meter race, the javelin and discus throws, a 1,500-meter race, a 110-meter high hurdle race, the shot put, the high and long jumps, and the pole vault. The pentathlon events were the 200- and 1,500-meter races, the long jump, and the javelin and discus throws. Tewanima qualified for the long distance 10,000-meter race.

There was great excitement when these events came up at the Olympic Games. Americans and Europeans alike were eager to see how Indians would do competing against athletes from around the world. Jim and Tewanima didn't disappoint the crowd. In his race, Tewanima finished a good second to a famous runner from Finland, winning a silver medal. Jim Thorpe won both the pentathlon and the decathlon, setting an Olympic record in the decathlon that lasted sixteen years.

Americans won sixteen gold medals, and two of those were Jim's. When King Gustav presented the medals to Jim, he said, "You, sir, are the greatest athlete in the world." Jim, of course, had never met a king, and he didn't know how to respond. He just said, "Thanks, King."

Jim and other athletes were treated as great heroes when they returned to the United States. Parades were held in New York and Philadelphia, and Carlisle spent an entire day celebrating. When the celebrations ended, school resumed, and another football season began. That season Jim made 25 touchdowns and scored 198 points, at that time the greatest number of points ever recorded by a college player. After the Carlisle-Brown game, a headline in the *Providence Journal* read, "The Real Score—Thorpe 32, Brown 0." Jim won All-American honors for the second year in a row.

The blow fell in 1913. A newspaper published a story about Jim's playing semi-pro baseball in North Carolina. The story came to the attention of the Amateur Athletic Union, the organization that was responsible for the United States Olympic teams. In those days, any athlete competing in the Olympics had to be an amateur. It was promptly decided that because Jim Thorpe had been paid for playing baseball, he was a professional athlete and had competed in the Olympics illegally.

Jim was publicly condemned for concealing his professional status. Jim hadn't understood those rules, but no allowance was made for that. His gold medals were taken from him and given to the second place finishers in his events. All mention of his records was removed from the Olympic record books.

In February 1913, Jim left Carlisle for good—nine years after he entered. He received offers right away from several big league baseball clubs. He signed with the New York Giants. Jim, however, wasn't very successful at professional baseball. He hadn't had enough playing experience to be the big star the club manager had hoped he would be. His name was a drawing card for a time, but Jim found more frustration than fulfillment in his professional baseball career.

Being a professional baseball player did provide certain advantages, as Jim discovered when he married Iva Miller in the fall of 1913. Iva, who was part Cherokee, had been a popular student at Carlisle. The newlyweds spent their honeymoon enjoying an all-expenses-paid goodwill tour around the world.

22

Two years later, Jim began playing professional football for the Canton Bulldogs. At that time, the best pro football teams were in the Midwest. The Bulldogs were headquartered in Canton, Ohio, where the Pro Football Hall of Fame is now located. Jim was able to play both football and baseball because their seasons didn't conflict and because training was not as rigorous as it is today.

Jim played baseball on minor league teams through 1920, but his real love was football. He never achieved the success he had hoped for in baseball, but he was a great football player. He could run, he could block, he could tackle, and he could kick. And the fans loved him. In 1916, he helped the Canton Bulldogs win the professional football championship. In 1919, he kicked the ball an amazing ninety-five yards for a winning field goal. Although it was aided by the wind, football fans called it the greatest kick ever.

In 1920, Jim Thorpe was elected president of the newly-formed American Professional Football Association, which was a forerunner of the National Football League. He was too easygoing to be a good administrator, however, and he didn't hold the position for long. He did continue to coach and play, though. In 1922, he organized the Oorang Indians, a team that included many of his football friends from Carlisle. The team played two seasons with some success and plenty of good times. Jim played until 1929 when he retired at the age of forty-one. By that time, he had lost many of his skills, but he never lost his ability to kick the football.

Jim's personal life wasn't as successful as his sports career. He and Iva divorced. Their first child, James Jr., died of influenza in 1918, and Iva and many friends thought that Jim never really recovered from the heartbreak of his son's death. Jim married two more times and had a total of eight children. He had never taken his education seriously enough to prepare himself for a good job after his athletic career. Over the years, he had many different jobs to support himself and his family.

When the Olympic Games were held in Los Angeles, California, in 1932, Jim sat in the presidential box with Charles Curtis, the vice president of the United States, who was also part American Indian. The 100,000 fans in attendance gave Jim a standing ovation. Such moments of public recognition were rare, however, and Jim was largely forgotten until 1950. In that year, the Associated Press conducted polls of sportswriters and broadcasters to determine the most important sports figures of the first fifty years of the twentieth century. Jim was selected as the best football player, and he was also selected by an overwhelming margin as the greatest athlete of the half century. Jim's newfound fame led to the production of a movie based on his life. It was called *Jim Thorpe—All American* and starred Burt Lancaster.

Jim died in California in 1953. His body was taken back to his Oklahoma birthplace for burial. When plans for a memorial there fell through, his wife decided to have him buried in Pennsylvania where he went to school. There, two neighboring towns—Mauch Chunk and East Mauch Chunk—merged and took the name *Jim Thorpe*. The new community built a marble tomb for the final resting place of the great American Indian athlete who began his glorious career at the Carlisle Indian Industrial School.

The National Football League named a most valuable player award in Jim's honor. He was named to both football halls of fame—professional and college. In 1982, the International Olympic Committee restored Jim's gold medals. His records were put back into the Olympic record books, and his outstanding performances were once again officially recognized.

King Gustav's assessment of Jim Thorpe was accurate. Thorpe was the world's greatest athlete, and his overall versatility was magnificent. It is fitting that one of America's greatest athletes was a descendant of the original Americans.

HISTORY OF JIM THORPE

1887	Jim Thorpe was born. Congress passed the Dawes Severalty Act calling for the break-up of Indian tribes and the division of tribal lands among tribal members.
1904	Jim Thorpe entered Carlisle Indian Industrial School.
1909	Jim Thorpe played semi-pro baseball in North Carolina. The National Association for the Advancement of Colored People was founded.
1912	Jim Thorpe won two Olympic gold medals.
1913	Jim Thorpe's Olympic gold medals were taken away because he had played semi-pro baseball.
1920	Jim Thorpe was elected president of the American Professional Football Association (a forerunner of the National Football League). The first city airport in the United States was opened in Tucson, Arizona.
1950	Associated Press named Jim Thorpe best football player and greatest athlete of the first half of the twentieth century.
1953	Jim Thorpe died. General Dwight D. Eisenhower became the thirty-fourth president of the United States.
1982	The International Olympic Committee restored Jim Thorpe's gold medals and his Olympic records to the record books.